Food and Recipes of the Westward Expansion

George Erdosh

The Rosen Publishing Group's
PowerKids Press™
New York

The recipes in this cookbook are intended for a child to make together with an adult.

Many thanks to Ruth Rosen and her test kitchen.

Published in 1997 by The Rosen Publishing Group, Inc.
29 East 21st Street, New York, NY 10010

First Edition

Book Design: Danielle Primiceri

Photo Credits: Cover (right) © Bettmann, (right) © Patrick Ramsey/International Stock; pp. 4, 7, 8 (top), 13, 14 (top), 16, 19, 20 (top) © Corbis-Bettmann; p. 10 © Bettmann.

Photo Illustrations: pp. 8 (middle, bottom), 14 (middle, bottom), 20 (bottom) by Ira Fox; pp. 9, 15, 21 by Christine Innamorato and Olga Vega.

Erdosh, George.
    Food and recipes of the westward expansion / George Erdosh.
      p.   cm. (Cooking throughout American history)
    Summary: Combines the story of the pioneers with recipes and the history of food from the opening and development of the American West.
    ISBN 0-8239-5115-4
    1. Cookery, American—History—Juvenile literature. 2. West (U.S.)—Discovery and exploration—Juvenile literature. 3. United States—Territorial expansion—Juvenile literature. [1. Cookery, American—History. 2. West (U.S.)—Discovery and exploration. 3. United States—Territorial expansion.] Title. II. Series.
    TX715.E666 1997
    641.5'0973'09034—dc21

                                                                                97-2574
                                                                                CIP
                                                                                AC

Manufactured in the United States of America

Contents

Heading West

Edward was ten years old in 1850. Like thousands of other people at that time, Edward's family were **pioneers** (py-un-EERZ). They were headed for an area of land in what is now called Oregon, on the west coast of North America. Many pioneers were looking for cheap, **fertile** (FER-tul) land on which to farm or raise cattle. But other pioneers were in search of **adventure** (ad-VEN-cher). They wanted to explore lands that were new to everyone but the Native Americans who already lived there.

Thousands of people packed up their belongings and traveled west across North America. They were looking for the perfect piece of land on which to settle.

Pioneer Food

The pioneers were the first **settlers** (SET-tul-erz) to travel west. The **journey** (JER-nee) from Missouri to California took between four and six months to finish. Edward's family traveled in a covered wagon that was pulled by horses. Edward's mother packed enough food to last for the whole trip. Some families that they met along the way could only afford to bring flour, cornmeal, bacon, coffee, sugar, and salt. Edward's family brought those **supplies** (suh-PLYZ), as well as beans, rice, canned fruits and vegetables, molasses, and beef **suet** (SOO-it).

Edward's family didn't have fresh meat until they reached the first buffalo herds in the Midwest. Then Edward's father hunted and killed a buffalo. His mother cooked some of the meat, and dried the rest to save it for the trip. Some pioneers also hunted deer, antelope, and birds. Others caught fish.

Many pioneers hunted buffalo for meat during their long journey. ▶

Cooking on the Go

On their journey west, Edward's family usually stopped along the trail to rest for the night. Edward's mother cooked dinner over an open fire every night. The only cooking tools she brought with her were a heavy iron kettle, a frying pan, a small pot, and a wooden spoon. The rest of the wagon was filled with food, clothing, and farming tools. Some families that Edward's family met along the way had a tiny woodstove in their wagon. That way the women could cook, bake, and even boil water while traveling.

Edward's mother learned new ways of making food while traveling. The roads on the wagon trail were not paved. Edward's mother sometimes used the rocking of the wagon along the rough and bumpy roads to help her **churn** (CHERN) butter.

Skillet Bread

1¼ cups milk
1 tablespoon lemon juice
¾ cup all-purpose flour
1 teaspoon salt
1 teaspoon baking powder
1 teaspoon baking soda
2 tablespoons cold vegetable shortening

HOW TO DO IT:

☞ Preheat the oven to 400° F.

☞ Make sour milk by pouring the milk and lemon juice into a small bowl. Stir and let it sit for five minutes.

☞ Sift the flour, salt, baking powder, and baking soda in a medium-size bowl.

☞ Add the cold vegetable shortening. Mix it with the flour by cutting it into tiny pieces with two knives.

☞ Add half of the sour milk, and mix the dough with your fingers. Keep adding sour milk and mixing just until the dough sticks together. Let the dough rest for five minutes.

☞ Lightly grease the bottom and sides of an 8x8-inch baking pan with shortening. Put the dough in the pan. Dip your fingers in flour and spread the dough evenly out in the pan.

☞ Bake for 35 minutes or until the top is brown. Serve warm with butter or jam.

This serves four people.

9

Settlers and Prospectors

Once the pioneers reached a place they liked, they settled there. Edward's family settled in what is now the state of Oregon. Edward's father learned that the land in Oregon was good for growing wheat and raising cattle. The rivers there were full of a fish called salmon. Edward's family raised cattle. They, and many others, sold the meat, as well as milk, cheese, butter, and other foods to the growing number of people settling in California.

Gold was discovered in California in 1848. Thousands of **prospectors** (PROS-pek-terz) traveled to California in search of gold. Many of the people who moved there were more interested in searching for gold than in growing or raising food. They were happy to buy much of their meat and dairy products from the people of Oregon.

◀ *Once settled, some pioneers became farmers. Others raised cattle.*

Searching for Gold

Edward's Uncle Paul was a prospector. Edward learned from his Uncle Paul that prospectors lived in a very different way than the settlers.

Uncle Paul lived by himself in a tiny cabin in northern California. He had few belongings, but he did own a frying pan and a kettle for heating water. He ate simple food that he called grub.

Like most prospectors, Uncle Paul did not have much money. He wasn't married, and he didn't like to cook. His meals were often made up of bread, canned beans, bacon, and strong coffee. As a treat, he sometimes ate canned sardines. Uncle Paul hardly ever ate fruit, vegetables, milk, cheese, or eggs. When he had the money, he bought eggs and milk in a nearby town. He also caught and ate rabbits, squirrels, and fish.

Most prospectors worked hard to find gold, but few had any luck. ▶

Prospectors' Grub

Uncle Paul cooked his meals in simple ways. He cooked canned food right in the can on his stove or over a fire. He even ate the food out of the can!

Uncle Paul had a special way of making bread. He opened a bag of flour and poured in some water. He mixed the flour and water with his hands to make a dough. He took the dough out of the bag and pulled off small, round pieces. Then he flattened the pieces and fried them in hot bacon grease.

Edward loved to visit Uncle Paul. He liked looking for gold. He also liked eating out of a can and eating fried bread!

Uncle Paul's Dinner

You will need:

4 slices bacon
1 16-ounce can of
   pork and beans
1 can of sardines,
   packed in oil
soda crackers

This was a
real prospector's dinner!

HOW TO DO IT:

☞ Fry the bacon in a medium-size frying pan until it is crisp.

☞ Take the bacon out of the pan and put it on a plate covered with a paper towel.

☞ Pour most of the bacon fat into an old can or jar. Leave a little on the bottom of the pan to flavor the beans.

☞ Put the pan back on the heat, open the can of beans and empty them into the pan. Stir until they begin to bubble.

☞ Open the can of sardines.

☞ When the beans are hot, pour some onto your plate.

☞ Put a few sardines and a few pieces of bacon next to the beans.

☞ Serve with all the soda crackers you can eat.

This serves one prospector.

Mining Camps

When prospectors found an area that was full of gold, a mining company would build a camp nearby. The company would then hire people to **mine** (MYN) the gold. Uncle Paul was never lucky enough to find much gold. But he lived near a mining camp. During one visit, Edward and his father rode into the camp to see what it was like. It was easy to get to the camp because the roads leading to it were flat and smooth.

The miners worked hard and they ate a lot. The camp had a real kitchen and a dining house with two cooks. The cooks made soups, stews, roasted meats, and boiled potatoes with other vegetables. They also baked fresh breads, pies, and cakes every day. For breakfast they made eggs, ham, bacon, toast, and hot porridge with canned milk.

◀ *Mining camps sometimes turned into small towns, complete with dining halls and general stores.*

The Cowboys' Chuck

The settlers and prospectors shared the West with cattle ranchers and cowboys. One year, Edward had a chance to visit his cousin, Sam, in Texas. Sam was a cowboy. He told Edward stories about **driving** (DRY-ving) cattle from the ranch to the market, nearly 1,000 miles away.

The cowboys called their food chuck. The very first cowboys carried their food with them in sacks that hung from their saddles. They usually brought bread, bacon, salt, and coffee with them. Many years later, cowboys traveled with a chuck wagon on these long drives. A cook drove the chuck wagon, which carried a large chest of food, as well fuel, water, pots, and pans. The cook traveled ahead of the cowboys and cattle. Each night, he parked at that night's camp. He had dinner ready when the cowboys arrived. The cowboys worked hard and were hungry by dinnertime.

The cowboys were tired and hungry after driving cattle all day long. ▶

Real Cowboy Food

On most days, Sam and the cowboys ate steak for breakfast, lunch, and dinner. Every few days, a cowboy killed a cow and the cook cut the meat into steaks. The cook used any leftover meat to make pot roasts or stews. When the meat was gone, a cowboy killed another cow.

Along with steak, the cook usually served red beans, which the cowboys called "**prairie** (PRAYR-ee) strawberries." He also served rice or potatoes, cornmeal mush, and biscuits or bread. Sam told Edward that sometimes the cook made a special treat—dried apple pie.

Red Beans 'n Rice

You will need:

2½ cups of dry red beans

1 medium onion, diced

2 tablespoons vegetable oil

½ teaspoon salt

½ teaspoon onion salt

½ teaspoon garlic powder

½ teaspoon pepper

4 cups water

2 cups cooked white rice

HOW TO DO IT:

☞ Soak the beans in a pot of water overnight. Drain them when you are ready to cook them.

☞ Sauté the onion in the oil in a medium-size pot until the pieces are almost clear.

☞ Add the beans, salt, onion salt, garlic powder, pepper, and water.

☞ Cook over medium heat. Bring the beans to a boil.

☞ Stir, and lower the heat. Simmer for two hours.

☞ Serve the beans over the cooked rice.

This serves about four people.

The Wild West

The opening up of the West was an exciting time for the United States. New states, such as Michigan, Oregon, California, and Texas, joined the United States. Settlers found what they were looking for: land for farming and raising animals. There were also plenty of animals to hunt and fish to catch. It seemed like there was enough food and land for everyone.

However, as pioneers moved west, they settled on land that once belonged to different Native American tribes. Most of these tribes were forced by the U.S. government to live on small areas of land called **reservations** (reh-zer-VAY-shunz). It was a hard time for the Native Americans.

The foods from these four groups of people—pioneers, prospectors, Native Americans, and cowboys—slowly blended together to create many dishes of the West.

Glossary

adventure (ad-VEN-cher) An exciting experience.

churn (CHERN) To beat and shake cream in a wooden container to make butter.

driving (DRY-ving) Making something move from one place to another.

fertile (FER-tul) Good for growing things in.

journey (JER-nee) A long trip.

mine (MYN) To dig into the earth to take out valuable metals.

pioneer (py-un-EER) One of the first people to settle in an area of land.

prairie (PRAYR-ee) A large area of flat land with grass but few or no trees.

prospector (PROS-pek-ter) A person who explores an area in search of gold.

reservation (reh-zer-VAY-shun) An area of area set aside by the government for the Native Americans to live on.

settler (SET-tul-er) A person who moves to a new land to live.

suet (SOO-it) Beef fat.

supplies (suh-PLYZ) The food and equipment necessary for people to live.

Index